Washington 1900

Library of Congress

Pomegranate

SAN FRANCISCO

Pomegranate Communications, Inc.
Box 808022, Petaluma CA 94975
800 227 1428; www.pomegranate.com

Pomegranate Europe Ltd.
Unit 1, Heathcote Business Centre, Hurlbutt Road
Warwick, Warwickshire CV34 6TD, UK
[+44] 0 1926 430111; sales@pomeurope.co.uk

ISBN 978-0-7649-3977-8
Pomegranate Catalog No. AA359

Pomegranate publishes books of postcards on a wide range of subjects.
Please contact the publisher for more information.

Cover designed by Lora Santiago
Printed in Korea

16 15 14 13 12 11 10 09 08 07   10 9 8 7 6 5 4 3 2 1

To facilitate detachment of the postcards from this book, fold each card along its perforation line before tearing.

*T*he Library of Congress is the nation's foremost research center for the study of the history of Washington, DC, and its collections pertaining to the nation's capital are the richest and most varied in existence. This book of postcards holds only a small sampling of the Washingtoniana photographs held in the Library's Prints and Photographs Division.

It is to history more than anything that Washington owes its rich photographic record. Since it became the nation's capital in 1800, the city has always been a magnet for those with causes to promote, messages to deliver, statements to make, and policies to influence. At the same time it has also been a hometown to its citizens and merchants, and many of the Library's Washingtoniana images are of everyday people and places typical of any mid-size city in the past hundred years.

WASHINGTON 1900

In a photograph commissioned by the J.E. Hanger artificial limb company, an artificial limb recipient ice-skates near the Washington Monument ca. 1873. Photograph by C.M. Bell.

Pomegranate • Box 808022 • Petaluma, CA 94975

355

WASHINGTON 1900

African-American schoolchildren at the Greenough statue
of George Washington on the Capitol grounds, 1899. From
the collection of Frances Benjamin Johnston (1863–1952),
one of the first women to achieve prominence as a
photographer.

Pomegranate • Box 808022 • Petaluma, CA 94975

WASHINGTON 1900

Claude Graham White flying his Farman biplane along
West Executive Avenue, Washington, October 1910.

Pomegranate • Box 808022 • Petaluma, CA 94975

WASHINGTON 1900

An electric baggage truck operated by a baggage porter at
Union Station, ca. 1907.

Pomegranate • Box 808022 • Petaluma, CA 94975

WASHINGTON 1900

Ninth and G Streets, N.W., northwest corner (present site
of the Martin Luther King Memorial Library), showing
Patent Office fence, ca. 1913.

Pomegranate • Box 808022 • Petaluma, CA 94975

WASHINGTON 1900
The fords in Rock Creek Park, Washington, D.C., ca. 1906.

Pomegranate • Box 808022 • Petaluma, CA 94975

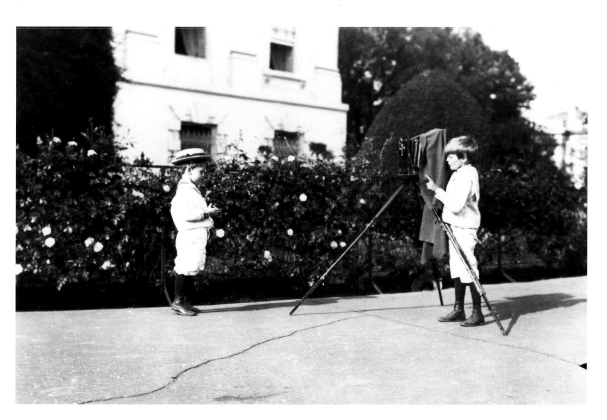

WASHINGTON 1900

Two of President Theodore Roosevelt's sons, photo-
graphed at the White House by Frances Benjamin Johnston
(1863–1952), one of the first women to achieve prominence
as a photographer, ca. 1902.

Pomegranate • Box 808022 • Petaluma, CA 94975

Prints and Photographs Division, Library of Congress

WASHINGTON 1900

White House kitchen, ca. 1904. Photograph by Waldon
Fawcett.

Pomegranate • Box 808022 • Petaluma, CA 94975

WASHINGTON 1900

Canal Street S.W. (or E Street S.W. and Maine Avenue),
Washington, D.C., ca. 1900–05, from a photographic
street survey of the city.

Pomegranate • Box 808022 • Petaluma, CA 94975

WASHINGTON 1900

Inmates with their Christmas tree at the District of
Columbia Jail, early 1900s.

Pomegranate • Box 808022 • Petaluma, CA 94975

WASHINGTON 1900

The Old Ebbitt Hotel, Washington, D.C., ca. 1885–95.

Pomegranate • Box 808022 • Petaluma, CA 94975

WASHINGTON 1900

Harvey, Baltimore & Potomac Railway Depot, Washington,
D.C., ca. 1897.

Pomegranate • Box 808022 • Petaluma, CA 94975

Fire Department
Washington

WASHINGTON 1900

Composite photograph of the D.C. Fire Department,
Washington, 1904. Includes montage group portrait,
portraits of chief and assistants, and photographs of
firehouses in the city.

Pomegranate • Box 808022 • Petaluma, CA 94975

WASHINGTON 1900

Dedication of the Washington Monument, Washington, D.C., February 21, 1885.

Pomegranate • Box 808022 • Petaluma, CA 94975

WASHINGTON 1900

Artisans at work on decorations for the interior of the Library
of Congress, July 19, 1894. Many of the plaster decorations
were created on the spot by artisans working in impromptu
studios in unfinished space in the new building. Photograph
by Levin C. Handy.

Pomegranate • Box 808022 • Petaluma, CA 94975

WASHINGTON 1900

U.S. commissioners and delegations of Sioux chiefs visiting
Washington, D.C., October 1888. Photograph by C. M. Bell.

Pomegranate • Box 808022 • Petaluma, CA 94975

WASHINGTON 1900

Right-hand section of a three-part panoramic view of
Washington, D.C., showing the Capitol (top left corner),
the Mall and Smithsonian buildings, and Southwest
Washington, ca. 1902. Photograph by Levin C. Handy.

Pomegranate • Box 808022 • Petaluma, CA 94975

WASHINGTON 1900

Currency wagon at the U.S. Treasury Department,
ca. 1906.

Pomegranate • Box 808022 • Petaluma, CA 94975

WASHINGTON 1900

Frances Benjamin Johnston (1863–1952), one of the first women to achieve prominence as a photographer, and her tintype studio at the Country Fair at Friendship, Washington, D.C., May 1906.

Pomegranate • Box 808022 • Petaluma, CA 94975

WASHINGTON 1900

Physical education class with weight-lifting equipment at
Western High School, Washington, D.C., 1899. From the
collection of Frances Benjamin Johnston (1863–1952), one
of the first women to achieve prominence as a
photographer.

Pomegranate • Box 808022 • Petaluma, CA 94975

WASHINGTON 1900

Center Market, Washington, D.C., early 1900s. Photograph by Frances Benjamin Johnston (1863–1952), one of the first women to achieve prominence as a photographer.

Pomegranate • Box 808022 • Petaluma, CA 94975

Prints and Photographs Division, Library of Congress

WASHINGTON 1900
State Department Library in the State, War, and Navy
Building, Washington, D.C., ca. 1900–05.

Pomegranate • Box 808022 • Petaluma, CA 94975

WASHINGTON BASE BALL CLUB.
1909.

WASHINGTON 1900

"Washington Base Ball Club," by the Barr-Farnham Picture
Postcard Company, 1909.

Pomegranate • Box 808022 • Petaluma, CA 94975

WASHINGTON 1900

White House Office telegraph operator, November 1909.

Pomegranate • Box 808022 • Petaluma, CA 94975

WASHINGTON 1900

Market Space and Pennsylvania Avenue, N.W.,
Washington, D.C., 1901.

Pomegranate • Box 808022 • Petaluma, CA 94975

WASHINGTON 1900

Interior of the dome of the Main Reading Room during
construction of the Library of Congress, October 1894.
Photograph by Levin C. Handy.

Pomegranate • Box 808022 • Petaluma, CA 94975

WASHINGTON 1900

Assembled gun, Washington Navy Yard, ca. 1905.

Pomegranate • Box 808022 • Petaluma, CA 94975

WASHINGTON 1900

Flooded Pennsylvania Avenue at Ninth Street, N.W., 1889.

Pomegranate • Box 808022 • Petaluma, CA 94975

WASHINGTON 1900

Pediment model being placed in position over the U.S.
House of Representatives portico in the Capitol,
Washington, D.C.

Pomegranate • Box 808022 • Petaluma, CA 94975

WASHINGTON 1900

The "Sight Seeing Automobile Coach of Washington,"
ca. 1905.

Pomegranate • Box 808022 • Petaluma, CA 94975

Prints and Photographs Division, Library of Congress